HI, MY NAME IS KHALIL JR.

I LIKE TO COUNT.

DO YOU LIKE TO COUNT?

COUNTING CAN BE FUN!

WE CAN COUNT TOGETHER.

ONE MAMA BEAR

1 HOUSE

2 TRUCKS

Two Pairs of socks

3

THREE APPLES

4 PAIRS OF SHOES

Four Furry 4 Friends

5 BUTTERFLIES

5 BOOKS

Six Hearts

6 TOOTHBRUSHES

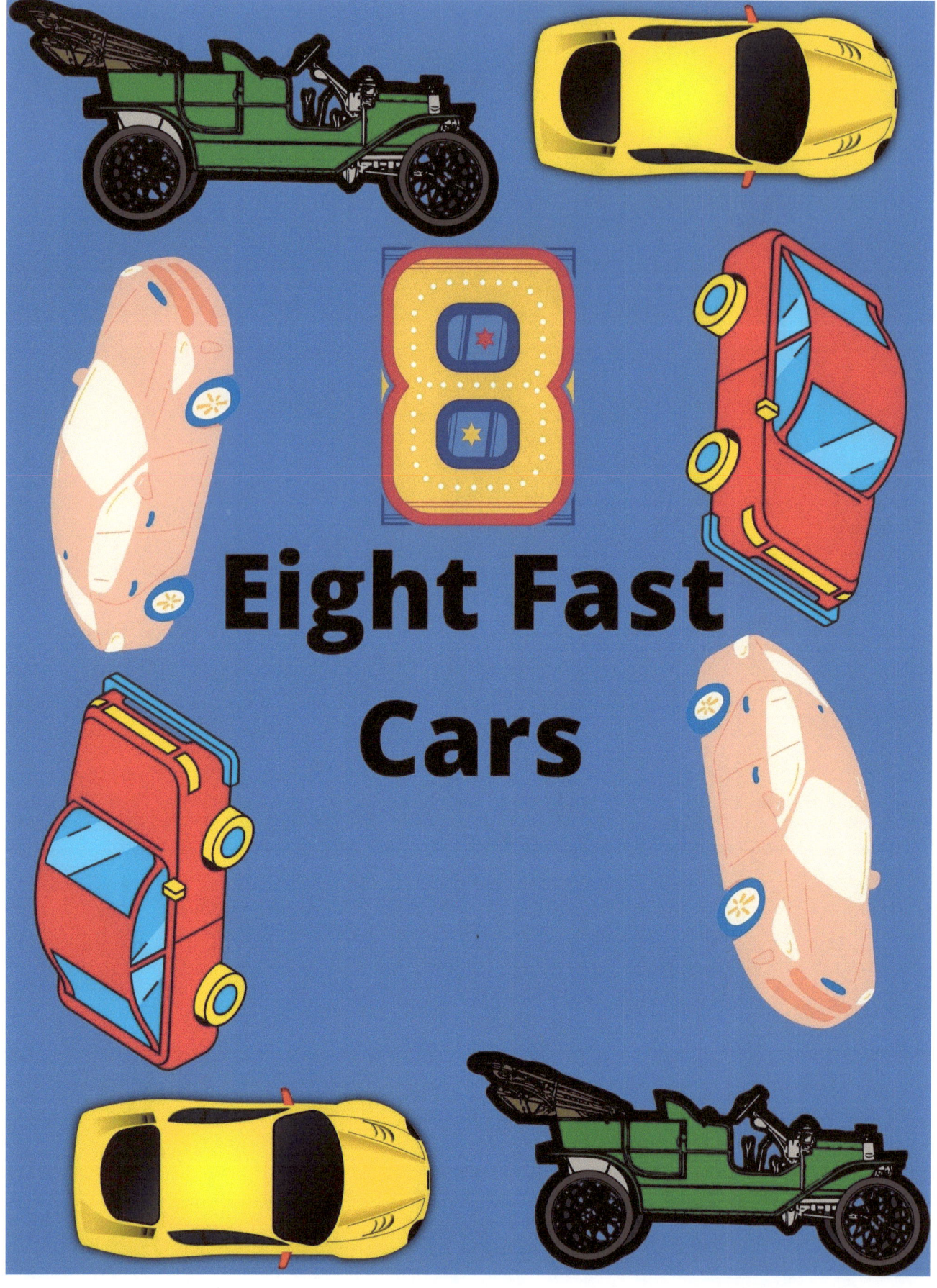

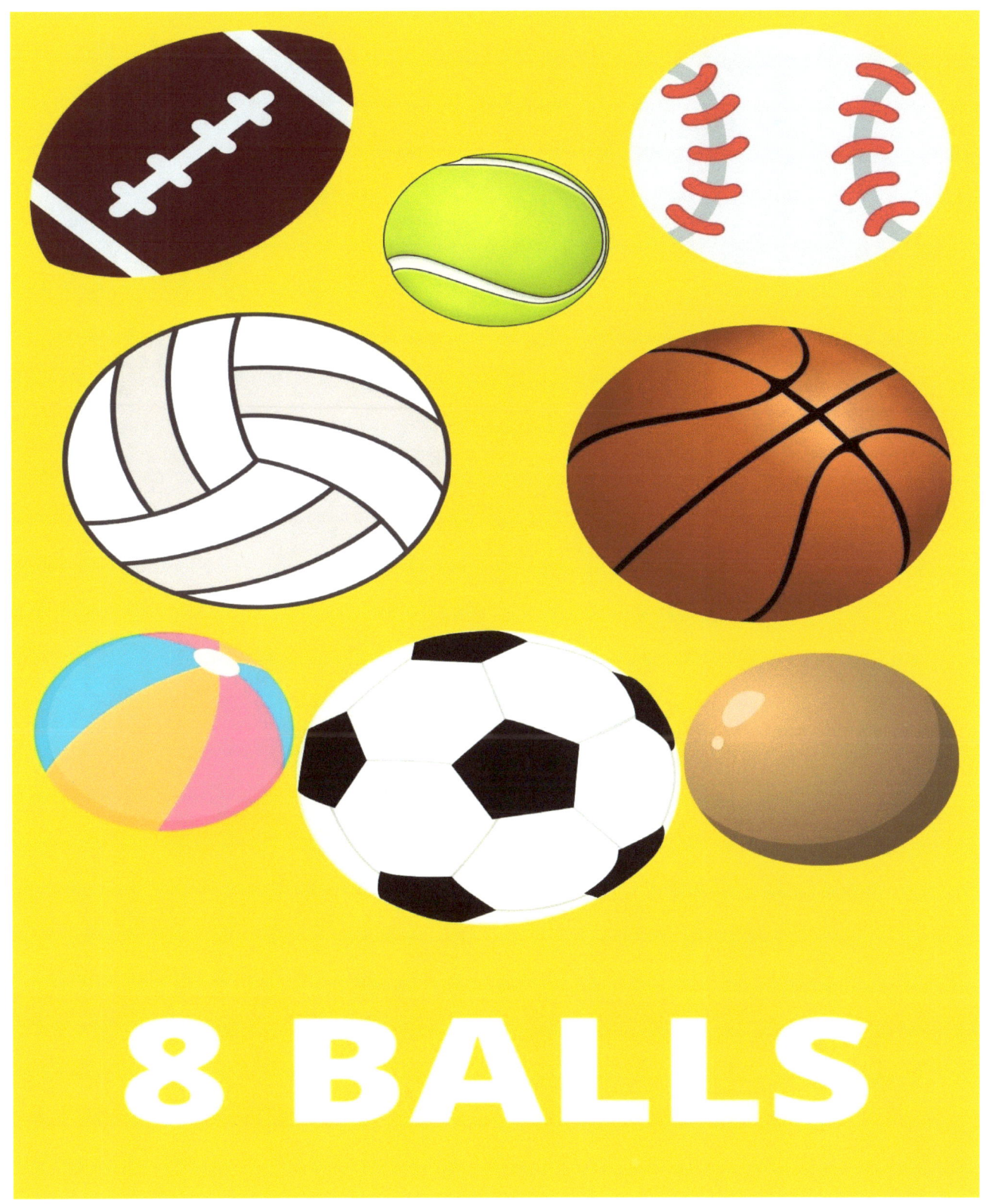

9 WORMS

Nine Balloons

10 LOTUS Flowers

www.ingramcontent.com/pod-product-compliance
Lightning Source LLC
LaVergne TN
LVHW072103070426
835508LV00002B/243